21 WAYS TO

DOUBLE YOUR PRODUCTIVITY,

IMPROVE YOUR CRAFT

& GET PUBLISHED

A Field Guide for Writers

by Writing Coach and Bestselling Author

Sara Connell

INTRODUCTION

I've been nourished by many great writing guidebooks. I've benefited personally and as a writer from Anne Lamott's *Bird by Bird*, Natalie Goldberg's *Writing Down the Bones*, and Heather Sellers's *Chapter After Chapter*. I've generated pages and pages of writing using the prompts in Bret Anthony Johnston's *Naming the World*.

Writing guides have fed me when the writing felt hard. They've shown me how to take the next step in my process. They've reignited my pilot light when I felt uninspired and began to doubt myself.

After a few decades of reading these beloved books and taking their counsel—a lone writer soul in need of guidance—I now have the privilege of coaching authors and teaching creative writing.

In this book, I've shared twenty-one ways I use myself and suggest to my clients and students to get unstuck, generate work, improve the quality of work, attract an agent, get a book contract, and get published.

There are many more than twenty-one techniques. We could do one hundred ways, or I could have drafted a *Moby-Dick*-sized writing guide, but that would be cumbersome and get in the way of the whole point of a writing guide—to get you writing!

So I've kept these entries brief (most of them) and divided the book into three sections: productivity, craft, and publication.

USING THIS BOOK

Feel free to go straight to the section where you most want to have a breakthrough. Or you can use the book as a writing intensive—a boot camp done over twenty-one days—the way we do in the writing jump start classes I run each fall. Find a technique you like and work with that one for a while until it's in your cells. Or go straight through the book and jump your writing career to the next level by implementing each "way" as you go.

To take what you read here further, I have free lessons, interviews, weekly video blogs, and insider tips at my website: www.saraconnell. com. I would be delighted to connect further with you and support you in any way I can!

Even if we never speak in person, please know that by picking up this book, we are linked in the magical chain of writer to writer. I hold the highest thoughts for you and your writing career. I believe in you and your calling, passion, and desire to write.

Thank you for entrusting me to be a part of your team. Without further delay, let's get to it. Let's get writing.

PRODUCTIVITY

1

WRITE YOUR GOAL

Studies show that if you think about a goal, letting it ramble around your head like a rock in a rock tumbler, you have about a 20 percent chance of achieving it. If you write a goal on paper or type it into your computer or phone, that number jumps to 60 perfect. So right now, grab a pen or pencil and some paper, or your phone or your laptop—typing a goal counts as writing it down. We'll talk about how to get that number to 100 percent later in this book, but first:

Write your Big Goal. What is the thing you'd love to experience more than anything in the area of writing? Is it publishing a novel, a children's book, or a perfect, beautiful poem? A memoir, the story your grandmother told you on the front porch of her house when you were little? Is your Big Goal writing a bestseller or being interviewed on Charlie Rose or Stephen Colbert? Or is your Big Goal writing that book that people just like you are going to read and it's going to change their lives? Or heal them? Or comfort them and make them feel—like all great writing does, in some way—that they are not alone?

Write your Big Goal now.

My Big Goal is _____.

ACTION: Place your Big Goal somewhere where you will see it every day. Read your Big Goal out loud every day in the present tense. See it, feel it, taste it, hear it. Like it's already happening.

2

YOUR WRITING GPS

To double our productivity as writers, we can approach our writing practice like a GPS. Without judgment, write down an estimate of how much you've been writing, on average, over the past month. This is your "current location." Haven't been writing? No problem. You write down 0. Five minutes a day? Five hundred words? As dispassionately as possible, write down your current location.

My current location is _____.

Your double productivity is your "destination." What does double-time look like for you? Is it to write for thirty minutes Monday–Friday this week? To write every day for seven days? Is it to lock yourself in a room or a cabin somewhere and not come out until you have that story written and polished and ready to send to *Harper's*? Is it to write 500 words or 1,000 words or finish a chapter or a draft? Is it to submit a piece for publication? To publish a story on your website? Identify your double productivity goal.

My double productivity writing goal this week is

_____.

Now, make it visible. Think of those reading challenges you might have done in elementary school, or a fundraiser thermometer chart—the kind that bursts out from the top when your organization hits the $10,000 mark. Let the inner kid in you have some fun with markers or crayons and draw an image you'll fill in each time you do a writing session. It's amazing how much you'll want to color in those empty circles or reach the top bar of that graph. If you want to get started writing and not making crafts, you can download a **double productivity template** here: www.saraconnell.com.

ACTION: Fill out the GPS coordinates above. Make a picture of your goal or download the template. Get writing! Fill in a section each time you succeed.

3

TIME

To increase productivity, we have to talk about time. Maybe Way #2 two wasn't helpful—yet—because you'd be happy to double your writing productivity but you don't know how to fit in the extra hours.

I use three time tools to double productivity:

TIME RECORDING

This tool is for people who don't have any time. You just don't know where you would fit in the writing. Most of us are not hermits or sequestered at residencies or monastic life. We have families, jobs, parents, siblings, schools, and communities all rightfully demanding our presence and engagement. We have to find a way to write *and* do these important things. Enter: the Time Log.

Today, log everything you do in fifteen- to thirty-minute increments.

7:00 to 7:15 shower
7:15 to 7:45 dress and eat breakfast

Log every single thing you do for a full week. Then, you'll look for opportunities—pockets and windows of time that previously went to things that are not as valuable to us as writing. Just like a food journal or money journal that enlightens us as to what we are really putting into our bodies or spending our precious dollars on, the time journal will show us the thirty-minute phone call that could've been finished in five minutes, the ten-minute trip to Target that lasted an hour, and the Netflix binge that could've satisfied us in thirty minutes but turned into five hours. There is no judgment in the time journal; we just write down what we do and look at it at the end of the week. If you do this and do not see an ounce of time to spare, there are the options of delegating a commitment, hiring or trading for some extra help, getting up earlier, or staying up later.

Doesn't the time journal TAKE time? It does, but I find the results outweigh the time expenditure. If your mind tells you repeatedly, "I don't have any time," this tool can create a shift. The time log is a high return-on-investment activity. The time log is also very boring. The good thing about the boredom of forcing ourselves to scrutinize the minutia of our daily activities is that you will want to get through this step as quickly as possible. The time log will send you running to your writing time.

ACTION: Log your time for at least one day—ideally, one week. Circle every place you could have engaged in writing versus another, less important activity. Get excited—you've just struck gold.

4

TIME SCHEDULE

One of my mentors drilled this phrase into my head: *What gets scheduled gets done.* Pick a time on Sunday or whatever day you like. Think of an appointment you would never miss—maybe it's the dentist, your child's school conference, or lunch with a good friend. Pull out whatever tool you use to schedule these important meetings—Google Drive? Paper calendar? Old Filofax? Chalk board in your kitchen? The iCal app on your smartphone? Whatever you use, book your writing time there. Every week, sit down for five minutes and block out your writing time for that week.

Remember: when we write something down, we are 60 percent more likely to achieve that goal.

ACTION: Schedule your writing time for the rest of this week in your calendar/device of choice. Read ahead to Way #6 to supercharge this strategy!

5

TIME WEDGES

A few months after my son was born, I attended a workshop in which a woman said she had completed three books writing entirely in thirty-minute time "wedges." She had three children under five and quickly realized she was never going to have the long stretch of the writing time she envisioned she needed to write one book, let alone three. But she's a writer and wanted to write more than she wanted to sleep or have a clean house or sit down to eat lunch. She knew she was very lucky to get the book deal—and by God, she was going to write those books. She finished every one of the three books on time. She's writing the fifth book now. She mastered the time wedge.

A teacher wrote his mystery novel by writing forty-five minutes every day during his lunch break—in his car. At 11:45, he left his classroom, carrying his lunch in a brown paper bag and a thermos. He rolled up the windows, cast his eyes on his laptop and didn't stop typing until the bell summoned the students back to fifth period.

The time wedge is a short increment of time where the dedicated (or desperate) writer can make real progress. A time wedge can be as short as ten minutes or as long as forty-five. Instead of scrolling through Facebook, reading news headlines, calling your father (you can call him after you write!), spending fifty minutes on Instagram, or strolling aisles at Whole Foods, pull out that notebook, laptop, or even your phone (you can dictate into notes and email the doc to yourself later). Find a wedge and pounce; in minutes, you'll move your writing project forward.

MASTER TIP:

To make the most of a time wedge, think about what you're going to tackle next. In the shower each morning or while brushing your teeth, identify the next scene, chapter, character, story idea, or poem you're going to write. Hemmingway reportedly stopped every writing session in the middle of a sentence. That way, he resumed writing the next day already in flow. Start dreaming, marinating, and steeping in your next idea while you drive to work or walk your kids to school. When the wedge comes, you will be ready.

ACTION: Pull out your time journal, if you made one. Identify any wedges of time you might previously have "thrown away." Notice any open wedges from the log or in your day today. Instead of reaching for your phone or other distracting activity, grab your notebook or laptop and write.

BONUS: Log every time you use a wedge to write. Celebrate yourself. Pat yourself on the back. Post it on our writers' Facebook group: https:// www.facebook.com/groups/389550031387146/?ref=bookmarks

You just took your writing to a new level. You just went pro.

6

ACCOUNTABILITY, BUDDY

I swam on a swim team from age four through my senior year of high school. Throughout my swimming years, my coaches would time my individual events (where I competed alone) and my relay splits (when I swam in an event with three other swimmers). My relay times were always faster. When I swam individually, I kicked what I thought was as hard and dragged my arms through the water until my lungs burned. I would have passed a polygraph saying I'd given everything I had to give in that individual race. And yet as I stood on that starting block, my blood would start to pump faster. Some additional fire would be ignited. I'd spring forward with a strength I didn't have on my own. Sometimes I'd swim half a second faster in a relay—in swimming terms, that's light years.

I've heard about the same phenomenon for runners, golfers, philanthropists, and members of sales teams. It's as if we humans are wired to do more, push harder, and go farther if we're committed to others than we will ever do for ourselves alone or on our own.

Remember we said that writing down a goal takes the likelihood of success from 20 percent to more than 60 percent. Having an accountability structure will take your percentage into the 90s—sometimes all the way to 100.

Your accountability structure can be a person, a friend, a writing group, a class, a coach, a mentor, a Facebook group—basically, anyone to whom you can name your goal and report on your progress.

Try it out. Identify an accountability structure/person who supports you and will hold you to your word. Try a few until you find the one that has you cutting seconds off your time and making the pages fly. Keep up your structure until you're holding your printed book in your hand, until you are looking at your book on the shelves of your local bookstore, until you see your book on the bestseller page of Amazon.

You've got this!

ACTION: Identify an accountability structure/person to hold you accountable to your double productivity goal this week. You can use my structure or make up one of your own.

Simple template:

1. Email or text your writing goals to your accountability buddy/buddies at the beginning of the day or week.

2. Do the work.

3. Email or text your actual writing numbers (time, pages, word count, and research time) when you finish.

BONUS: Ask your partner to send you celebratory emojis. You can use our Facebook Group as an accountability buddy, too: https:// www.facebook.com/groups/389550031387146/?ref=bookmarks

I'll be cheering you on all the way!

7

PLEASURE BUNDLING

Have you heard of the podcast *Freakonomics*? I listen to a lot of NPR in the car, and one day *Freakonomics* featured a researcher named Katherine Milkman, who'd conducted a human behavior study at the Wharton School. Milkman took a group of people who really wanted to do something but were unable to do it. (Can you relate?) In this case, it was exercise, but you can think about the study in terms of writing. These people really wanted to make healthful choices in their lives but were unable to go to the gym, or an exercise class, or even take a walk.

The study worked like this: The participants each made a list of their favorite things to do—things that they did for pure pleasure—HBO shows, romance novels, some kind of art or craft, dinner out with friends, etc. Next, they signed an agreement that they would do the activity only WHEN, or right after, they exercised. The research team assumed the participants would achieve a higher exercise rate when motivated by their desire to get to the pleasurable activity.

They did. The participants' exercise rate went up 80 percent from the 0–5 percent it had been at the start of the study. Some of participants followed through with 100 percent of their exercise commitment. That's neat, right? We can incentivize ourselves into doing more writing by giving ourselves something easy to do, something we love to do, right after. It's neat, but not revelatory.

However, something revelatory did happen. The participants didn't start to exercise more just to get the reward of the pleasurable activity. By linking the difficult-to-do activity (in our case, writing) and the fun, enjoyable activity, their brains began to rewire themselves. The same positive feelings of anticipating and doing the pleasurable activity began to fire in the brain when the person prepared and engaged in the previously difficult activity. The people began to like exercise—*for the exercise.*

Sometimes, it's hard to sit down to the page. It can be hard to tackle a revision. Send out an article. Craft a query letter. Write a synopsis. It can be hard to post about our writing and ourselves on Facebook, film an author video, or sit down and write again.

But we can bundle these activities with something delicious and wonderful. We can move through resistance. We can get more done. And then, as if by magic, the difficult thing might become our bliss.

ACTION: Make a list of three things you LOVE to do. Ideally, these would be things that are overall positive activities for you. Drinking margaritas or eating ice cream can be great but if they have a negative backlash (if you suffer from them or feel shame), leave those off the list. For one week, commit to watching that show, calling that friend, listening to that podcast, or taking that walk in the forest preserve only WHEN you've completed your writing. Feel your neurons and synapses begin to change. Pleasure your way into your success.

If you're interested, here is the Milkman study. She calls it temptation bundling: https://www.facebook.com/groups/389550031387146/?ref=bookmarks

IMPROVE

YOUR

CRAFT

8

COPYING

When fine art students (painters, sculptors) begin their training, teachers send them to museums to sketch the "masters"—Picasso's bathers, Brancusi's fish, Cézanne's pastel landscapes of the South of France with their marvelous cubist shapes. It is expected that the way to become good is to imitate—to attempt—by tracing pencil over paper in the shape of genius. Visual artists are instructed do this over and over again, like alchemists turning base metal into gold.

I don't hear writers being told this often. And yet, just like the painters, we writers can make huge leaps in our craft by turning to a masterwork—a novel, a poem, one glorious sentence. We can sit at its feet, as if on holy ground, and move our hands across the page in those same keystrokes, the same consonants, vowels, and arrangement of words. As we do, we are not just thinking about the words we copy; they come through us, and our hearts begin to beat with their rhythm. The brilliance that created them begins to fire in our own brains. We do this practice and hope that by repetition and the magnificent generosity of the universe, we will become it for a moment, and it will work its way into our writing.

ACTION: Identify a master writer (any writer you love or admire). Select a favorite page, paragraph, scene, or sentence. Pull out a piece of paper and copy it exactly. Feel your pen or fingers on the keyboard, and let yourself be taken over by the genius.

9

WRITE EVERY DAY: DEVOTE YOURSELF TO A CONSISTENT PRACTICE

A number of years ago, I was at a turning point. I felt a hunger to fully dedicate myself to writing, but I wasn't sure what "fully dedicating myself" meant. So I did what I'd coached many of my clients to do in their various fields: I read biographies and memoirs and listened to interviews of authors I loved and of successful authors from all genres. After three weeks of reading, a single common denominator emerged: every successful author had a consistent, diligent, devoted writing practice. They all wrote often. They all wrote a lot.

Some writers espouse the lifestyle: write every day. Stephen King famously wrote in his memoir *On Writing* that he "only takes off Christmas and his birthday, but actually he writes those days, too." I read these books and decided that to be a good writer, I must write every day, too. If I didn't, I would never become the writer I want to be. But there are very successful authors who do not write every day. Rebecca Makkai, who consistently makes it into *Best American Short Stories* and is on her third successful novel, says she takes time off—sometimes weeks—when she's in a particularly busy teaching or book promotion schedule.

A professor I know from Northwestern University teaches during the school year and writes from May to September. At the moment, I'm in a "writing every day" period. But this past spring, I was taking an intensive literature class, running a business, parenting a six-year-old, and involved in a few family projects. For the sake of my sanity (and my family's) I took four weeks off to write the literature papers. Other life obligations can easily become excuses not to write at all, so I made a deal with myself: I would take three weeks off writing to devote myself in integrity to those tasks, and then I'd write my butt off this summer.

I used to think I had to be in a good mood, be "inspired," have the right pen, the right room, total silence, or just the right amount of ambient noise. For those of us who are lifelong writers, for those writers who want to get writing done, we may need to loosen these conditions. There is a point (the point when you go professional as a writer) when you will be able to write in a gas station rest stop if that was the only way you were going to get your writing done that day. I've written short stories in doctor's office waiting rooms, revised pages of my novel in line to pick up my son from school, drafted an essay while sitting on a folding chair at the beach.

Now, I make my writing schedule at the beginning of each week. If I miss a day, I make up the time the next day or on the weekend. and DO IT.

There is no way to become a successful, published author if we don't write. In her wonderful guidebook *Crash Course: Essays from Where Writing and Life Collide*, Robin Black says, you can't get to the good pages if you don't write the ones you don't like. It doesn't have to be every day. You might write more in the winter or more in the summer. Pick something. Stretch yourself and devote yourself to writing, consistently, devotedly. Write every day or every three days or most days—whatever stretches you while still being manageable—while still being kind to yourself and the people in your life. Before you know it, you'll be one of those authors you love. Before you know it, you'll be sending out stories and flash fiction and prose poems and entire books for publication. You'll believe that you are a "real writer". You'll be a pro.

ACTION: Pretend you totally believe in yourself. Pretend writing is your job. Write today. Make a schedule for the week and follow through. Do whatever you need to do to write often and consistently. Repeat.

10

FIND A MENTOR

Not a single piece of writing that has been traditionally published was entirely created by the writer alone. Every great author (that I know of) at some point worked with an editor or writing group, teacher, professor, or coach. We don't think of this often when we start out. We think writers are supposed to sit down, churn out a perfect, beautiful, polished piece of writing in one sitting, and then sit back to bask in the awe of critics and readers.

Writing, in actual fact, is nothing like this. Anne Lamott gave us the language of "shitty first drafts." Verlyn Klinkenborg of *The New York Times* said, "All writing is revision."

We need extra sets of eyes on our work. If we're going to be successful professional authors, we'll need to get feedback from wise, skilled, loving eyes and revise the work so it can gleam.

I avoided this step for years. I wrote, sometimes literally, in the closet. I wrote pages and chapters and once a full novel, but I couldn't show them to anybody. The thought of someone telling me what was wrong would kill me, I thought, or at least stop me doing this thing that I desperately wanted to do. I still don't enjoy getting feedback every time. But something I can offer is a reframe.

What if instead of people telling us what's wrong with our work, we can think of feedback as the chance to work with angels who are here to make our writing better? Getting feedback and revising our work is not a sign that we didn't do it right or that we're not "good." That myth is the talk of the Inner Critic—the Gremlin. The Inner Critic is like those internet trolls who post anonymous hate and never give their real name. Getting feedback on your work means you're serious about writing. It means you're a professional. It means you're going to go all the way.

I do best with mentors and editors who are honest and also supportive and encouraging. When I give feedback, I do so with the mindset of one of my mentors, who says, "Everything can be delivered with kindness." You might be a tough love kind of person. You don't care how the message is delivered; you just want the good stuff—the move, the cut, the new ending that will make your writing sing. Invest in this part of the process. Avail yourself of the alchemy that comes from getting feedback, so you can revise your work and stretch yourself to new heights. Great writing does not happen in isolation. It was never meant to.

ACTION: Share your work. Find a person, group, teacher, mentor, coach, or class who knows something about writing, whose work or teaching style you admire, and send a piece of your work. Take the feedback notes that resonate for you and revise the piece. Congratulate yourself. You just took a leap forward toward your vision. Your readers will thank you. You'll thank yourself. You're becoming the full writer you were meant to be.

11

CRAFT LECTURES

We're told to "read like writers," but often, especially early on, we don't know how to accomplish this task. If the writing is good, we get seduced by the story. We don't watch "the man behind the curtain" for long. When we do, we don't know what to make of what we find there.

How did that author make me want to stay up reading until two o'clock in the morning? How did that writer show the character's backstory without using a single flashback?

A craft lecture is a talk prepared by a writer and usually focusing on an element of writing craft, typically in one particular work. Tension-filled dialogue in Hemingway's "Hills Like White Elephants," use of time in Alice Munro's "Tricks," the lyrical prose in James Joyce's *Dubliners*, or the epiphany ending in Walter Kirn's "Planetarium." Ranging from five minutes to two hours, the craft lecture is revelation, a skillful guide, someone who knows, lifting the curtain and breaking down the story into digestible bites that we can turn to gold in our own writing.

The Colgate Writers' Conference posts craft lectures on YouTube. Without leaving your computer screen, you can watch craft lectures by Jennifer Egan, Junot Díaz, George Saunders, Stuart Dybek, and Dani Shapiro. You can listen to Ann Patchett and Jamaica Kincaid. If you want to treat yourself, try Rebecca Makkai's two-part lecture at the University of Kentucky on "endings."

Craft lectures are not the same as author interviews. I love interviews and listen to them for inspiration and motivation. But craft lectures are where I go when I want to take my work to a new level. Craft lectures will deconstruct a story, a novel, a sentence, or a single, beautifully chosen word. These lectures can help you go from amateur to professional. You can apply one nugget from each lecture to improve everything you write. Craft lectures are the food that makes your writing grow. If you let them, they will take you to mastery.

ACTION: Type your favorite author's name + craft lecture into YouTube or Google. Watch one craft lecture and write down a technique, move, or trick you want to try. Pull out your computer and give it a go, applying your new genius to your writing.

12

STEEPING

Good writers must read widely and prolifically. Francine Prose says that if a student reads closely enough, they'll know how to write well. I was an English major in undergrad. I won the MS Readathon every year in grades 1–8. I easily consumed a book a day on a vacation with my family in the summers, reading late into the night when everyone else was asleep while the ocean lapped against the sand outside my window. I'd have loved this to be the whole training, the only action I needed to take to become a writer. Reading until I burst with inspiration, then churning out beautiful, wrenching prose—a riveting, finely tuned story. It was not. It is not. I did not have Francine's rapt and tuned way to process the writing I read yet. I don't believe, for many of us, reading alone will get us all the way to becoming the writers we want to be, but I do believe reading can gigantically improve our craft.

I recommend a particular kind of reading that I call steeping. Similar to copying, you'll pick a book, story, or poem (whatever you most want to write) and then read it. When you get to the end, read it again, over and over, as many times as you can. Read the page or paragraph or novel. Read it aloud. Sleep with it next to your bed. Read more things like this book. Underline or highlight or dog-ear the parts that make your chest tingle, your spine straighten, your fingers twitch to get to your keyboard. Steep in the words, the rhythm, the tone, the staggering poetic language of the authors who arouse in you the almost painful calling to write. Read a story a day, a book a week. Like copying, if we steep in the good stuff long enough, it will come out in our writing. You'll see new metaphors, dialogue, and some of those staggering descriptions crackle on your page. Steep in it long enough and you'll become one of the greats—one of those geniuses you admire.

ACTION: Challenge yourself for a month to read a story, poem, or chapter a day of the kind of writing you most want to do. Read it once, and then read it again. STEEP. Hang suspended in the words. Let them soak into the folds of your brain, into your bone marrow. Then write for fifteen minutes.

13

SHOW

If you take an intro to writing class, likely the first thing you'll hear is "Show, don't tell."

If we compare a section of exposition (where the writer tells the reader what is happening) to a section written in scene (where the writer shows the reader what is happening), we'll see writing in scene is usually more riveting, compelling, and exciting.

In a research study, neuroscientists hooked readers up to electrodes and found that when a reader reads good, full sensorial writing (writing that shows), the same centers in the reader's brain light up as if the reader were actually experiencing what was being described.

So we don't work and toil and struggle to SHOW in our writing just to torture ourselves. We SHOW because it's the service we provide the reader; we show to fulfill the promise we offer when they crack the spine or swipe open the cover of our story—to take them to another world, another time, into the very soul of our characters or ourselves.

One of my writing teachers gave her students the goal to write in 80 percent scene and 20 percent exposition. Most early first drafts come out inverted. We're still telling ourselves the story, so we have long paragraphs or pages of explanation and backstory. We give a "day in the life," show the childhood bedroom, that awful moment when the character's parents said they are getting a divorce, that embarrassing moment at the prom. Our intuition tells us to draw readers aside and tell them about the people and setting and story so they'll care—so they'll keep reading. Then we find out we have to flip the pyramid.

How do we do this? We write scenes, ideally in the present action of the story. We slyly pepper in the foreshadowing and backstory, and demonstrate the stakes through dialogue, action, and obstacle. Like a fantasy lover, we seduce the reader into caring, into continuing to read, until they can't *not* read what happens next. We do this through the skill of our craft.

Imagine if a writer wrote, "They went to the Amazon and did research," instead of showing us neon glowing frogs in the jungle and microscope slides where hormones formed ferns on the clear, thin glass. Writing like this doesn't just show the reader the scene; it creates a world so real, so pulsating, the reader is IN the scene. Your readers don't want to just hear about the ship; they want to board the craft and walk the plank. They want to feel the spray of salt sting their faces. They want to LIVE the story.

ACTION: Read through a draft of your current project. Check the following:

1. Are you 80 percent scene, 20 percent exposition? If not, try a revision to get closer to that ratio goal.

31

2. Find a paragraph that isn't popping the way you'd like. Rewrite to use sensory and intimate, specific detail.

3. Watch your writing gleam like a pro.

GET

PUBLISHED

14

THE SUCCESS MINDSET

A few months ago, I was preparing to send out a new short story for publication. I read and revised the story many times. I'd received feedback from professors in my MFA program and had several savvy writer friends provide edits. I'd received positive comments on this story from these trusted advisors. I thought the story was good. And then, when I uploaded the file, suddenly my mind filled with dialogue something like this:

This isn't very good.

It's not good enough for this journal.

The structure is weak. I don't have a strong enough predicament.

This story won't win a contest.

I don't have the skills to publish at this caliber of magazine.

Can you relate to this episode?

In coaching we call this a "gremlin attack": a barrage from the critter brain, the inner critic whose entire job it is to stop us from succeeding at our dreams.

Before we send out our work, it can be beneficial—even crucial—to elevate our mindset. The work can get published even if we don't believe in ourselves, but I believe our mindset is a piece of an overall strategy for success. It's a bit like the adage about not being able to be loved until we love ourselves. If we want others to praise and value and publish our writing, we can start with praising and valuing and loving our writing ourselves.

It can be difficult to love our writing. If we've taken a few workshops or classes, our ears may be tuned to find the flaws, the ticks, the "problems." It's good to find the cracks, the plot holes, and the flat characters or dialogue. We find them and get the mentoring we need to revise and to heal those broken places so the story can sing. Then, once it's done—once we've given it everything we've got—we turn to the good.

To instill a success mindset, I offer the following exercise: First, read the draft of your current story, poem, or chapter and write at least five things that are great about it. Keep going. Write down everything that is working, every startling, original idea. Send this list to yourself in an email or a text. Read it at least five times before you send out your piece. Know that the story does not need to be perfect to be published. Celebrate your effort, your growth, your courage, and your perseverance. Celebrate the five-plus things on that list. Envision the editor or publisher gravitating toward your submission. Imagine the people reading your work sparking to your ambitious prose, your knack for simile, the surprise reversal in your plot.

ACTION: Every time you prepare to send out a piece for publication, make a list of five great things about your writing. Look for every opportunity to praise and validate your talent. Love your writing first, then watch as the world follows. Bring on the fan mail.

VISION BIG, START SMALL

What is your ultimate publication credential? Where do you dream of seeing your name in print? I met a woman who said if she didn't get into *The New Yorker*, she didn't want to be published. I love thinking big. I admired her commitment to excellence—no settling. *The New Yorker* or bust.

AND I'm not sure the go big or go home strategy serves all of us writers.

When I started out, I was just desperate to be published. I wanted into the club. I was self-taught. I knew no one in publishing and had no literary connections. I was working at a holistic clinic during the day and writing before or after work. One day, the owner of the clinic was offered the chance to write a column in a new wellness magazine that was starting up. My boss didn't want to touch it. "I know we *should* do it," she said. "But ugh, writing." I shot up my hand like Hamilton. The owner of the clinic said I could have the column. The deal was done. I had my first published piece.

We never know where opportunity will reveal itself. While you're listening for your big break, consider the smaller stones that will build a bridge between your current location and the *New England Review*. I created a list of 10 PUBLISHING HOT SPOTS (see below) you may want to try. These are places beyond national magazines and the very top-tier online journals. *Salon, The Huffington Post, The Atlantic*—all great, but thousands of publications need content. Print, online, mobile friendly, 120 characters. People, organizations, businesses, and publications need writing—good, professional writing—and you can be the one to fill them. Starting small, going for the opportunity nearest you and doing it again and again; building with each publication credit and byline, one small step at a time, paradoxically becomes another way to play big. Cast a wide net, start small, and you'll be in the big leagues in no time.

10 PUBLISHING HOT SPOTS:

1. Alumni magazines—Find out if your past schools (elementary school through university) have a magazine and if alumni may pitch/publish articles. Think about pitching a "where are they now," article, an essay on changes in life and technology since you were a student, or a profile on a classmate who is changing the world.

2. Small business newsletters—Most small business send out newsletters online. Most of these entrepreneurs are not writers. Offer your expert services to write or edit their content and you'll likely find yourself enveloped in gratitude and with a stack of publishing clips to share with future editors and agents.

3. Charitable and not-for-profit journals and blogs—Like small businesses, NFPs often publish journals and blogs. Have you volunteered or contributed to a charitable organization? Do you share a passion for protecting animals or cleaning up the environment? A writer I know who is now on her second novel got started this way. You get to be of service to a cause and develop your publishing chops. Everyone wins.

4. Guest blogging on other people's blogs—Many blog authors seek out other writers to contribute. They'd love to feature someone who will take on a topic that inspires their readers. Scroll through the blogs to which you subscribe. Email the writer and pitch a short post you think will add value to their message/topic.

5. Your own blog—Think of a book you may some day want to write and begin posting riffs on that topic in short 500-word posts. Instant publishing cred.

6. Cause-based journals—Have you survived a trauma, battled an illness, or succeeded in a twelve-step recovery group? Many cause-based organizations have journals and newsletters, both local and national, and are often looking for content.

7. Parenting organization websites—There are hundreds, if not thousands, of parenting organizations. Many have online newsletters, publications, and blogs. Pitch them a funny piece about dealing with backtalk or a provocative piece on how to instill grit (the buzzword at the time I'm writing this book). Parenting organizations are looking for good, quality content that will inform and entertain their readers. Go for it.

8. Conferences publications—Conference often publish newsletters and online journals throughout the year to engage readers

between events. Pitch a piece about attending your first conference, a "behind the scenes" with key speakers, or whatever would delight you to write. Your name will be associated with the conference, with those authors. Very exciting.

9. LinkedIn—Articles are big business on LinkedIn. Articles with numbers in the title and tip based articles such as "5 biggest mistakes to avoid when interviewing" and "The #1 insider secret that will land you a literary agent" get widely circulated and lots of traction.

10. Social media—Publish your thought of the day, first line of a story, or a social rant. Instant gratification, fast response, and in minutes you're a writer with an audience. This seems obvious—it's the forum for the masses, and everyone can publish on social media. Everyone can, BUT people share posts. They retweet. Bloggers and agents and publishers read social media, too. I know more than one author who has been contacted by a writing professional because of a social media post. Get out there! Get posting!

ACTION: Write out your Top Vision List—the places you'd most like to see your story, novel excerpt, memoir chapter, or poem appear. Paste it up on your computer or your bathroom mirror, your refrigerator, or the door of your closet. Then choose one publishing hot spot from the list above and email the person in charge of content. Send an email with a story idea, submit a poem, or offer to guest blog for a friend. Vision Big, Start Small. It works.

16

ONE HUNDRED SUBMISSIONS

Last year, Lit Hub ran an article about an author who boasted that she'd aimed for "one hundred rejections per year." Ouch, you'd think—how awful. But what the story revealed, once you read on, was the way the author ingeniously freed herself from rejection shame. When she made one hundred rejections her goal, she freed herself from paralysis. She vastly increased her number of submissions. She took her power back. She also got published. Yes, she received many rejections, but she also had three pieces published, was invited to a reading series, and was awarded a residency (a paid time away for writers, usually somewhere beautiful in nature, where you write, write, write). She was living the dream!

Inspired by this author's tenacity and scope, I hosted a writer's challenge with my colleagues, students, and clients. Everyone set a submission (not publication) goal, and we worked together, cheering each other on, to submit one hundred pieces (or whatever number they chose) in one year. I didn't have the, well, balls yet to aim for one hundred rejections. But I could focus on one hundred submissions. Focusing on submissions is like focusing on your training in a sport versus focusing on winning the game. Focusing on the action (rather than the outcome) makes us strong. It burns down the ego and shows us what we're supposed to be doing: writing the best work we can and sharing it as boldly as we can with the world. You'll stop caring so much about any one response. You won't have time. You have one hundred submissions to send out! The bonus is that you'll have more writing published. By the end of this exercise, you'll be a pro.

ACTION: Set a number of submissions goal for your work. Start sending out work. Maybe one this week. Three next week. Then five, then ten. You can find a wealth of journals, magazines, and online publications at Duotrope and in *Writer's Market* and Writer's Digest (www.writersdigest.com).

Click here to read the whole one hundred rejections article: lithub. com/why-you-should-aim-for-100-rejections-a-year/

17

SUBMITTING

Before I coached writers and wrote full time, I worked as a life coach. When someone came to me for advice on being in a romantic relationship, we took a three-pronged approach. I recommended online dating, following their passion by taking classes or attending events they already loved, and asking everyone they knew to set them up on dates. I attended eight weddings in two years. The three-pronged approach worked.

When approaching writing submissions, I take a three-pronged approach to publication as well: the three-legged stool. The first leg is general submitting—submitting online and via email to journals, magazines, agents, and publishers. The second leg is pitching live at conferences or other writing events. Third, networking: attending the readings, meetups, live events, online chat rooms, writers groups, and lectures that will fill us, inspire us, and just might land us sitting next to the person whose connection will get us published.

I'll discuss pitching and networking in upcoming "ways."

For this lesson, I've included some overall dos and don'ts for general submitting. For book length projects, you'll write a query letter. You can download a query letter template I use at www.saraconnell.com. Query Shark gives great advice on writing queries as well: www.queryshark.blogspot.com.

For literary journals (ideal for short stories and poetry), you'll write a cover letter. The cover letter simply states the name of your piece, the word count, a sentence or two about you, and any publication credits. Many journals publish work from new authors, so no concerns if this will be your first published piece.

I've read for Northwestern's literary magazine and talked to many editors and contest judges. Here is a cumulative list of best practices for query letters and cover letters:

DO:

- Be brief.
- Proofread everything. Many of these guys will reject a submission if there are typos.
- Be courteous.
- For queries, customize each letter. This takes work, but it will pay off big time. Every author I've worked with who has been published or received a book deal this year has taken the time to research what else the agent/editor has published. Show them you took the time to learn a little bit about them and their agency/publication. Doing this will take you to the top of the pile.

DON'T:

- Overshare, such as giving your birthdate, hobbies, or life traumas (I have seen cover letters with each of these).
- Tell the editor, agent, or publisher that you are a great fit for them. Instead, write that you were inspired to query them because they represented _____ books or _____author.
- Take it personally if you don't get a yes. There are thousands of agents, thousands of editors, and thousands of journals—a whole universe of opportunities to publish. You will find your match.

18

NETWORKING

Every writer I know hates this word. I did, too, but networking is the next leg of the stool I use to get published. Sometimes you'll get published through the "slush pile" (the general submissions sent to an agent, publisher, or magazine). That's why one hundred submissions is the first leg of the stool. But for the stool to stand, we want to have two other legs standing strong. For you to get your pieces consistently published, we're going to mine your network: family, friends, colleagues, and random people you meet at the grocery store or on the street, at exercise classes or writing classes, or at family reunions.

You're going to start asking everyone you know: "Do you know any agents, publishers, magazine editors, or book editors?" We never know whose second cousin is now the acquisitions editor at Penguin Random House or runs a small but well-respected literary magazine in Vermont. This action is not always much fun. Networking requires you to summon a colossal amount of humility and harness the drive deep in your gut that makes you want this thing called publication enough to level your ego and find the courage that every person who decides it's time to start dating does when they ask all their friends to set them up.

When I finished my first manuscript, I came to the upsetting realization that I had not a single literary connection, not a single personal lead to whom I could send my work. It took me over six months of asking, but one day my husband's stepfather mentioned one of his clients had published a book. I took a swig of water, set it down unsteadily on the table, and asked.

I followed up a few more times. On a Friday in April, Roger called. He'd found the name of the agent who represented his client.

"She won't by any means necessarily represent you, but she will talk to you. I've got one shot with this woman. Are you ready?"

I wasn't, of course. The minute I faced the reality of being on the phone with a literary agent, I thought everything in my book was crap. I felt like I should claw my way underground somewhere for another six years and keep working on the memoir. But I showed up for the call. The agent took my call. She is still my agent seven years later.

There are other ways to network, too, such as author readings, book signings, lectures, writing conferences, and festivals. A friend of mine spent one full day walking the aisles of an annual writing conference where publishers from all over set up booths in a football-field-sized convention hall. She asked the editors of the publications what they were looking for from authors. My friend offered any connections she had that might benefit their publishing goals. She went home and sent one of her best stories to each publication, with a sentence at the top of the cover letter that said, "It was lovely to meet you at AWP." After several years of rejection letters, that year, after networking in person, she had her first three stories published.

If networking still sounds awful, think about networking as "following your passion." Go to the conferences that tickle your ribs when you think about attending. Follow your passion to the events featuring wonderful authors reading their staggering prose. Fill yourself with lively discussions that will not only yield wonderful connections but will send you racing to your computer to write. Follow your passion right into becoming published.

ACTIONS:

1. Ask everyone you know if they know an agent, editor, or publisher—or anyone who knows anyone who might. Politely contact these people and say you have a book, short story, poem, or article and would be grateful if you could send it to them.

2. Scour poets and writers magazines' conference editions, your local online listings, meetups, literary organizations, and bookstores. Make a list of every event you'd genuinely like to attend. Then GO! Not every event will nurture and inspire you. Not every conversation will lead to a connection. If you're nervous, focus on how you can help the people you meet as much as they might be able to help you. Focus on generosity and gratitude. Focus on your vision. This may be the way you get published. The event may lead to your breakthrough.

19

PROCESSIONAL EFFECT

Does this all feel like a lot of work? Do you feel fatigued even thinking about researching publications, customizing one hundred cover and query letters, and staying strong through rejections and motivated during the revision process?

Here's something that helps me:

One of my mentors, Eric Lofholm, talks about a phenomenon called "the processional effect." The processional effect says that every positive action we take toward our writing goal will have an equal or greater positive effect. But he also says that the equal effect will not always be evident at first. The positive outcome is not always linear. We may go to a conference and not have an authentic or breakthrough connection with anyone. We may send out one hundred queries and not get a yes right away. Because of this, the processional effect is vital. It promises us that our effort will pay off—that positive result will come.

I don't know how your brain works, but my mind's first reaction to this idea is *Please*—as in "Yeah, right." When I take an action and don't get an immediate and desirable result, my response is to think the *no* or the lack of engagement is evidence I am a terrible writer and don't deserve any success. I should just give up now because, after all, what is the point? There are thousands of writers who are already beloved and succeeding at this publishing thing—prolific, likely far more talented, disciplined, and connected.

My mind offers this unhelpful hate speech, this even though I know I have witnessed the processional effect. I've experienced it. A writer with whom I worked this year received her book contract the day she sent her 101st submission. My book deal came not from the first book I sent to my agent (the one with a ninety-three-page book proposal with detailed chapter outlines—the one I worked on for three years) but from my second book, which sold in three days to a publisher who'd read that arduous ninety-three-page proposal, liked it, but rejected it in the nicest way, saying, "It's not right for us."

The processional effect can look like you submitting to ten magazines and getting your piece published not by any of those magazines but by someone your neighbor introduced you to after he found out you were a writer at your annual block party.

I heard a woman on a panel last year tell the story of how her novels were rejected for nineteen years. Nineteen years! She told her husband that when she hit twenty years, she would pack up her computer and retire. She'd take up something else—swimming, macramé, or coin collecting. A colleague suggested she self-publish and, in what she thought was a silent swan song, she uploaded her first book on Amazon. In three weeks, she'd sold over one thousand books. In three months, she'd sold over ten thousand, and readers were asking rabidly for her next book. She was easily able to oblige them. She'd written more than fifteen novels in those two decades, and every few months she uploaded the next one through a self-publishing company. At the time of the panel, she'd made over a million dollars from the sale of her books. One million dollars. Publishers were hounding her to print second editions. People wanted interviews. "An overnight success!" someone said when they blogged about her. "One night plus nineteen years," she said to the panel.

Nothing we do in service of our vision is wasted. Every action—writing, submitting, networking, dreaming, sketching, creating, supporting another author, posting work online—not only counts, but it moves you forward to the achievement of your goals. You may think your writing session today or the story you send to the slush pile of that little-known magazine is as silent as a tree falling unobserved in the woods. You may think your work makes no sound. We feel this way until we get that acceptance letter, the book contract, or the email with subject line "Congratulations!" But your action is not a silent tree. You action is a mighty force with wind and traction and results in the future beyond what you could imagine.

Every action counts and every action moves you further toward your goal.

ACTION:

1. Make a list of the actions you would take today if you knew you would succeed. What and how much would you write? Where would you submit your work? With whom would you reach out and connect?

2. Take the action that stretches you the most. Double down. Take the two actions that stretch you the most and release any expectation of the outcome. Know that you've logged a tick mark in the giant cosmic counter. You've moved your writing and your career forward.

3. Keep going and don't be surprised when the results come. Let us know when the breakthrough happens. We can all rejoice and be inspired and delighted by the how.

20

FUTURE PULL

When a friend of mine was applying to medical school, she asked seven of her closest friends to write acceptance letters from her top-choice schools and send them to her through the mail. We got really into it. I looked up the name of the dean of admissions and pasted the school logo to the top of the paper. One by one, the letters arrived and she hung them by a string above the desk and looked up at them as she wrote her application essays.

I wouldn't learn the name of this technique until later, but what my friend had us do is called a Future Pull. A future pull is any activity that puts us in the experience of our future goal happening *now*.

Did you know the subconscious mind (the place where obstacles to our goals reside) does not distinguish between imagination and reality? The subconscious mind responds to repetition and imagery; it responds to emotion. If you suggest something with emotion and imagery strongly and consistently enough, your brain will believe it is happening. It will accept the new reality—the achievement of your goal—as fact.

Elizabeth Gilbert wrapped published books from her parent's shelves with handmade covers of the books she intended to write. Jim Carey wrote himself a check for $1 million when he wasn't even able to rub two coins together from his stand-up comedy. I sent myself emails from "my agent" when hardly a soul had read my work. I mocked up a book contract with legal language I pulled from the internet. I pasted my name into the contributor's page of magazines I love, a photo of myself with Oprah, and my future book title onto the top of bestseller lists.

If I placed the mock-up images next to the real magazine articles, book contract, and emails from my agent, you would have a difficult time determining which was which. You can see the picture of me with Oprah on my website. I've had clients lay their future pull emails and their actual book contract emails side by side. They're incredibly similar. Occasionally, the actual publisher email uses the same language or phrases as the future pull.

A future pull alone will not get you published, but future pull + writing every day can.

Be prepared for push back on this one. Your conscious mind will think you've lost your sanity. Your inner critic will laugh at you. But I tell you: I've seen this technique work more magic than anything, aside from the essential sitting down every day and crafting our work. People can laugh, and the inner critic can stare. But they'll all open up their mouths in surprise when you rub the future pull flint against the rock of your work and create fire.

ACTION: Decide on a future pull action that amuses you. Do one this week. If you really want to accelerate your success, future pull yourself every day for a month.

21

STEP INTO SUCCESS

To complete our twenty-one-way journey I offer this exercise to reinforce your success mindset. A terrific time to do this is just *before* you send out your work for publication. By doing this inner exercise first, we send the work into the world with more confidence, with enthusiasm, and we become undeniable. To set your success mindset, I offer an exercise from my mentors Stacy Morgenstern and Carey Peters, two black belt guru coaches in the field of habit change and success.

(If you want to hear this exercise guided, I've recorded it for you at www.saraconnell.com).

Find somewhere quiet where you can spend five minutes or so. Take a few breaths into your chest and then stomach, in through the nose and out through the mouth. Once you feel your shoulders drop a bit, think of a writer who has done what you want to do—maybe published several bestsellers, brought a new idea or paradigm to the world, crafted a story so riveting you read the book in one sitting and on the same day ordered everything else he or she wrote.

Now that you have your hero writer in mind, take a step forward and imagine you are now standing in that author's body. You're seeing with his or her eyes, breathing with his or her lungs. This will seem goofy, inane, a waste of time, but stick with me—this kind of work can move things, change things, and dissolve the blocks between you and your success.

What does this person believe about the world and her/himself that allowed her/him to achieve this success? Stand there for a moment and listen for what your mind offers you. Now breathe in and out again a few times, "trying on" what it feels like to have accomplished these wonderful feats.

Next, step forward again. This time, imagine you are in a warm, shimmering circle of light. The light can be golden or white or any color or no color at all. Feel the perfect warmth, the tingle of energy against your skin. This is the circle of space and time where you have also achieved the greatness you desire. See the blueprint. See the place where it has become a reality. You're there. You have written those books, soared to the top of whatever lists or awards to which you aspire, and touched the lives of hundreds, thousands, or more.

Ask yourself what you now know/believe about the world and yourself that enabled you to achieve these goals. Let the answer(s) rise to the top of your brain or the center of your heart.

Imagine looking back to the you who had not yet stepped into the circle, had not yet achieved these literary heights. What is the most important quality, action, or thought needed to bridge the space between where you are now and the you standing in the circle? What do you want that emerging you to know?

Walk back to the spot where you started. Stomp your feet. Breathe in and out a few times. Feel and know you've taken back with you all you need to reach that space in the circle. Stand in your circle as many times as you need, maybe every day for a week, until you *feel* it. Until you know it—the writing, the publication, the success, is already done.

ACTION: Pat yourself on the back for not gagging (too much) as you tried something as New Age as "visualization." Pretend it was all worth it, that you just spent the most valuable five minutes of your writing career. You just might have.

CONGRATULATIONS on showing up for this twenty-one-day/way adventure! You rock. You likely came to this book with some ninja ways of your own. If you'd like to share, you're invited to share your tips with our ongoing group "More Ways to write more, write better, and get published" list at www.saraconnell.com and connect with other writers, find more tips, and listen to insider interviews with publishing experts in our Facebook group.

It's been an honor to be with you. I envision your greatest writing success and fulfillment from here. Keep going. Keep writing. GO!

Sara